Fact Finders®

CAUSE AND EFFECT: AMERICAN INDIAN HISTORY

Apache Resistance

CAUSES AND EFFECTS of Geronimo's Campaign

BY PAMELA DELL

Consultant:
Brett Barker, PhD
Associate Professor of History
University of Wisconsin–Marathon County

CAPSTONE PRESS
a capstone imprint

Fact Finders Books are published by Capstone Press,
1710 Roe Crest Drive, North Mankato, Minnesota 56003
www.capstonepub.com

Library of Congress Cataloging-in-Publication Data
Dell, Pamela.
 Apache resistance: causes and effects of Geronimo's Campaign / by Pamela Dell.
 pages cm.—(Fact finders. Cause and effect: American Indian history)
 Includes bibliographical references and index.
 Summary: "Explains Apache resistance under Geronimo's leadership, including
its chronology, causes, and lasting effects"—Provided by publisher.
 Audience: Grades 4 to 6.
 ISBN 978-1-4914-4836-6 (library binding)
 ISBN 978-1-4914-4904-2 (paperback)
 ISBN 978-1-4914-4922-6 (ebook pdf)
1. Apache Indians—Wars—Juvenile literature. 2. Geronimo, 1829-1909—Juvenile literature.
3. Apache Indians—Kings and rulers—Biography—Juvenile literature. 4. Apache Indians—
Government relations—Juvenile literature. I. Title.
E99.A6D37 2016
979.004'9725—dc23   2015009999

Editorial Credits
Catherine Neitge, editor and designer; Bobbie Nuytten, designer;
Eric Gohl, media researcher; Karina Rose, production specialist

Source Notes
Page 11, line 4: Debo, Angie. *Geronimo: The Man, His
Time, His Place.* Norman: University of Oklahoma
Press, 1976, p. 38.
Page 17, Fast Fact: "Old Apache Chief Geronimo
is Dead." *The New York Times.* 18 Feb. 1909, p. 7.
16 April 2015. http://timesmachine.nytimes.
com/timesmachine/1909/02/18/101733916.
html?pageNumber=7
Page 23, line 4: Hirsch, Mark. "Too Long a Way Home:
Healing Journey of the Chiricahua Apaches." American
Indian. Summer 2008. 16 April 2015. http://blog.nmai.
si.edu/main/2011/05/too-long-a-way-home-healing-
journey-of-the-chiricahua-apaches.html

Page 26, line 5: Jackson, Ron. "Stories of the Ages:
Geronimo." *The Oklahoman.* NewsOK. http://ndepth.
newsok.com/geronimo. 16 April 2015
Page 27, line 19: "Native Americans blast bin Laden
code name." NBC News. 4 May 2011. 16 April
2015. http://www.nbcnews.com/id/42897871/ns/
world_news-death_of_bin_laden/t/geronimo-native-
americans-blast-bin-laden-code-name/#.VOIihlo74yA

Photo Credits
Alamy: North Wind Picture Archives, 10; Capstone: 23; Charles Deering McCormick Library of Special
Collections, Northwestern University Library: 28; Collection of Jeremy Rowe Vintage Photography,
Vintagephoto.com: 12; Corbis: 26; Courtesy of Jeroen Vogtschmidt: cover, 7, 17; CriaImages.com: Jay Robert Nash
Collection, 9, 18; Getty Images: Stringer/MPI, 21, Time Life Pictures, 13; Library of Congress: 5, 14, 15, 16, 25;
Newscom: Picture History, 19, ZUMA Press/JT Vintage, 22; Shutterstock: Everett Historical, 24; SuperStock: 11
Design Elements: Shutterstock

Printed in Canada.
052015   008825FRF15

Table of Contents

The Great Warrior
GERONIMO

A baby with a great destiny was born in about 1823. He was given the name Goyahkla, meaning "one who yawns." But as this young Apache grew up, he came to prove his name false. He became known as Geronimo, one of the fiercest warriors in American history.

Geronimo was born into the Bedonkohe **band** of the larger Chiricahua Apache tribe. The Bedonkohe Apache lived in a part of Mexico that today is southeastern Arizona and western New Mexico. Geronimo came into manhood in troubled times. By the 1850s American Indians of the Southwest had long been at war with the Mexicans. Now they faced a new threat. American settlers, explorers, **prospectors**, and government troops began moving west onto Apache lands.

Along with other tribe members, Geronimo fought these enemies. But in the early 1850s a single terrible event set the course of the young warrior's life. From that time forward, Geronimo dedicated himself fully to fighting the Mexicans and then the Americans. His long bitter struggle made Geronimo's name impossible to forget.

The first photo of Geronimo was taken in 1884. Various spellings of his name included Goyahkla and Goyathlay.

band—group of related people who live and hunt together
prospector—person who looks for valuable minerals, especially silver and gold

What Caused GERONIMO'S CAMPAIGN?

In the 1800s Indian territory was being threatened on all sides. Geronimo's war was part of a wider American Indian rebellion against people taking their lands. Three main causes triggered Geronimo's long-fought **campaign** across the Southwest.

Cause #1: Centuries of Conflict

For centuries before Geronimo's birth, the Apache and the Mexicans had fought viciously for land, resources, and justice. The Apache frequently swooped in to raid towns in the Mexican states of Sonora and Chihuahua. The Mexican government could not stop the attacks.

The Apache lived in the Southwest's rugged mountains and deserts. Food and other supplies were hard to come by, so raiding was an accepted part of Apache culture. Geronimo became a warrior by age 17. He almost certainly joined in raiding from that time on. The Apache went after weapons and livestock, especially horses. They murdered and took **hostages**, as did the Mexicans. The Mexican government paid a **bounty** to anyone who killed or captured an Apache.

The Apache had no choice but to go on raids to survive as more and more of their land was taken over.

FAST FACT

Legend says that the Mexicans shouted *"Cuidado*! (Spanish for "Watch out!") Geronimo!" whenever their Apache enemy appeared. This may have been their version of the name Goyahkla. But some historians think the Mexicans were calling for protection from St. Jerome, which is Geronimo in Spanish.

campaign—series of battles fought in one region

hostage—person taken by force and held, often as a way to obtain something

bounty—money offered for killing or capturing someone

Cause #2: Mexican Massacre

To avoid raids, the Chihuahuan government in Mexico began giving the Apache food **rations** in early 1851. But on March 5, a band of Mexicans rode near Janos, Chihuahua, to hunt down Apache. That day Geronimo and other Apache men had gone into Janos to trade. Their wives and children remained camped a few miles outside town with a handful of warriors to guard them.

On their return to camp, the Apache traders found that a **massacre** had occured. More than 20 men, women, and children had been slaughtered. The Mexicans also took 62 prisoners, stole goods, and destroyed the camp. Among those lost were Geronimo's mother, wife, and children. The young warrior had lost his entire family in a single day. This murderous act set Geronimo off on a relentless campaign of his own.

FAST FACT

Geronimo was born at the headwaters of the Gila River near the border of Arizona and New Mexico. After officially becoming a warrior, Geronimo married Alope, a young woman from the Nednai band of Apache.

Cause #3: White Invasion

Following the Mexican War (1846-1848), the United States ended up with a large area of the Southwest. Much of this new U.S. territory was Apache homeland, but few Americans considered this.

Throughout the nation, American settlers were rapidly invading Indian lands, including Apache territory. Many whites treated the Indians harshly. In the Southwest people felt unsafe in their small **frontier** communities, fearing American Indian raids.

To make matters worse, rich deposits of silver, copper, and other minerals had been found in Geronimo's homelands. White prospectors swarmed over native lands, hoping to stake a claim. As the power struggles for land intensified Geronimo refused to back down.

ration—a person's daily share of food
massacre— the deliberate killing of a group of unarmed people
frontier—the far edge of a settled area, where few people live

American settlers who were headed west disrupted the lives of American Indians.

INDEPENDENCE
and Determination

In the early 1860s, Geronimo raided with the great Bedonkohe chief Mangas Coloradas and his son-in-law, Cochise. Mangas Coloradas was caught by Army troops in 1863 and killed. After his death, Geronimo hid in the hills and raided with various Apache bands.

Throughout the 1860s the Apache drove settlers from their homes, stole livestock, and fought back against Army attacks. Geronimo and his people hoped to drive all whites out of their lands. They felt their land had been taken illegally. After years of this constant warring, however, many Apache leaders considered making peace with the U.S. government. Geronimo was not one of them. Dealing with the loss of his family, his rage against the enemy burned on.

The Apache took aim at settlers, hoping they would leave their lands.

In Frederic Remington's painting Dash for the Timber, *American Indians chase prospectors from their land.*

Strange Prophecy

Geronimo was known as a fearless warrior. Perhaps this is why.

Sometime after the Janos massacre he claimed he heard a voice call his name. The voice told him, "No gun can ever kill you. I will take the bullets from the guns of the Mexicans, so they will have nothing but powder. And I will guide your arrows."

Geronimo often took dangerous risks in battle, but this **prophecy** proved true. Although he was often wounded, bullets did not kill him.

prophecy—something that a person says will happen in the future

Capture

Geronimo was called to a meeting on April 21, 1877, at Ojo Caliente, a New Mexico **reservation** also known as Warm Springs. He was to meet with John Clum, a government official in charge of the San Carlos Reservation in Arizona. Geronimo and several chiefs arrived, along with many others.

Clum accused the men of raiding, murdering, and stealing livestock. With the help of 100 armed Apache policemen, Clum disarmed Geronimo and the others and placed them in chains. For the first and only time in his life Geronimo was captured.

John Clum (center) and Apache scouts at the San Carlos Reservation

Soldiers stood guard as Apache men dug ditches at the San Carlos Reservation.

The Apache prisoners were taken to the San Carlos Reservation, a journey of several hundred miles. Arriving in late May, the so-called **renegades** were locked up for three months.

Although out of jail, Geronimo was not totally free. He had to live on the San Carlos Reservation. Life there was far from ideal, but many Apache were tired of running and fighting. Geronimo, though, wanted to live as he always had, free to roam the land. He and his family and several friends fled the reservation in summer 1878 and headed for Mexico.

reservation—area of land set aside by the U.S. government for American Indians; in Canada reservations are called reserves
renegade—someone who rejects lawful behavior

On the Run

Geronimo's freedom did not last long. In early January 1880 he gave up and returned to San Carlos. His breakout—followed by surrender—was not to be Geronimo's last. He escaped again in September 1881. Geronimo continued to resist the government's efforts to force him and his fellow Apache to live on reservations.

In April 1883 a military officer well known to the Apache began to track Geronimo. General George Crook was respected for making fair deals with the Indians. But his goal in Arizona was to capture Geronimo and get all the Apache onto reservation land. Crook caught up with Geronimo in May. Geronimo surrendered and returned again to the San Carlos Reservation.

Geronimo in Mexico's Sierra Madre Mountains

Geronimo and Naiche, chief of the Chiricahua Apache, posed on horseback in 1886. Perico, one of Geronimo's best fighters, held a baby. Geronimo's son Tisnah stood at right.

In spring 1885, however, Geronimo heard rumors that he might be hanged. He took flight again on May 17. By now the government had had enough of Crook. He was replaced in 1886 by Brigadier General Nelson A. Miles. Though Geronimo did not know it, the end of flight was near.

Final Surrender

By the 1880s Geronimo had the full attention of the American public. General Miles was determined not to fail in capturing him as other military leaders had. He appointed Lieutenant Charles Gatewood and several Apache **scouts** to track him.

Geronimo and his followers were an embarrassment to the government. They kept eluding capture while being pursued by as many as 5,000 soldiers. That was one-fourth of the entire U.S. Army.

The going was rough for Gatewood and his men. But on August 25, 1886, the scouts discovered Geronimo's hidden camp in the mountains of Mexico. The Apache warriors agreed to meet with Gatewood in another location. The Chiricahua trailed in. Finally Geronimo himself appeared. He laid down his Winchester rifle and shook hands with Gatewood. He agreed to come in and discuss terms with General Miles.

General Nelson A. Miles

scout—someone who travels ahead of a military group to gather information about the enemy

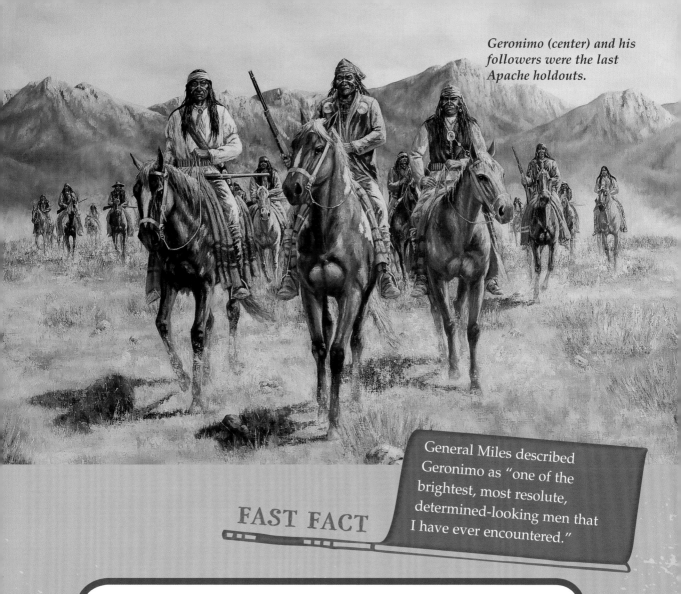

Geronimo (center) and his followers were the last Apache holdouts.

Geronimo was wary. But he was also tired of being in constant conflict and flight. So, on September 3, 1886, Geronimo surrendered at Skeleton Canyon near the Mexico border. Miles promised him that the Chiricahuas would have their own reservation. Families would be together. He said Geronimo would have farmland, a house, and livestock. He would not be punished for his past deeds.

Prisoners of War

Miles lied. The Apache who surrendered were shipped east by train as prisoners of war. Families were separated. Geronimo and the other "hostiles" were taken first to San Antonio, Texas. After 40 days the warriors were sent to Fort Pickens on an island in Pensacola Bay, Florida. Women and children were sent to Fort Marion, 300 miles (483 kilometers) away in St. Augustine, Florida.

Geronimo (front, third from right) and Naiche (front, fourth from right) and their followers were shipped by train to a Florida prison.

Geronimo (from left), Naiche, and Mangas, son of Mangas Coloradas, in captivity at Fort Pickens in 1887

Conditions were worse in both prisons than on the reservations. The Apache faced filth, lack of food, extreme humidity, and crude, cramped living quarters. Starvation and disease, including tuberculosis, took many lives. Some infants born in prison lived only a few days. By 1889 nearly 120 Chiricahua Apache had died at Fort Marion.

Eventually the Apache were reunited at Mount Vernon Barracks in Alabama, where their conditions improved. But Geronimo's dream of returning home was never to be.

What Effects Did GERONIMO'S CAMPAIGN HAVE?

Geronimo's resistance had many effects on him, his people, and on the wider American culture.

Effect #1: Lifelong Prisoner of War

After his final capture, Geronimo lived the rest of his life—22 years—in the **custody** of the U.S. government. He was both admired and feared. Many Americans, especially those in Arizona, did not want him ever set free. The settlers did not trust that the great warrior was "reformed" enough to live peacefully among them. If he returned, he would be killed.

Instead of being allowed to go home, Geronimo and the other Apache prisoners were moved to Fort Sill in October 1894. The Army post was in the Oklahoma Territory. In the end, Geronimo accepted his life at Fort Sill. Even though it was not their traditional home, the Apache began rebuilding their lives. They began to farm and raise cattle.

custody—imprisonment

Geronimo and his family raised melons at Fort Sill.

Forever a Captive

Geronimo and his fellow Chiricahua Apache were prisoners of war longer than any other American POWs on record. Geronimo was still in captivity when he died. He was thrown from his horse on a freezing winter night in February 1909. He was not found until the next morning. Geronimo contracted pneumonia and died February 17 at Fort Sill. He was buried there, in the fort's Apache cemetery.

Effect #2: The Apache Divide

After Geronimo's death, the remaining Apache at Fort Sill were still prisoners of war. They faced great pressure from U.S. Army officials, businesspeople, and politicians who wanted Fort Sill land for their own uses. The Apache were offered their freedom if they would give up their claims to the land. Many Apache resisted once again being pushed out of what had become their home. The land near the fort had been promised to them as a permanent reservation.

Some Fort Sill Apache stopped resisting in 1913. They had been prisoners of war for 27 years.

Apache scouts also lost their freedom.

FAST FACT

The U.S. Army betrayed the many Apache scouts who helped them track Geronimo. The scouts were promised they would be paid and receive land for their services to the country. But after Geronimo's capture, they were also imprisoned.

In what became known as "the Parting," they were relocated to New Mexico to live with the Mescalero Apache on their reservation. Those remaining at Fort Sill were settled on small, poor tracts of land north of the fort. In the new homesteads, the Fort Sill Apache lost the unifying force of living together. "Yet we survived in spite of everything," said the curators of an exhibition about the Chiricahua Apache at the National Museum of the American Indian. "We kept our values and our traditions, no matter what."

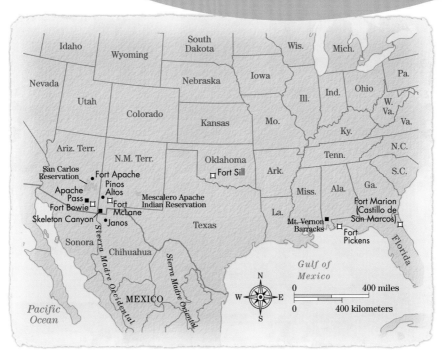

The Apache were moved from the Southwest to Florida and Alabama and back.

Effect #3: Famous American

The American press made Geronimo a household name. At the Mount Vernon Barracks, hordes of tourists came to meet the mighty and now renowned Geronimo. The old Apache was friendly to the visitors. He gave them autographs and sold photographs of himself.

Once he was removed to Fort Sill, Geronimo's fame increased. Artists painted his portrait. Photographers took his picture. Journalists wrote stories about him.

Geronimo also began to travel, accompanied by military guards. He appeared at large public events such as Nebraska's 1898 Trans-Mississippi and International Exposition. Geronimo appeared in an exhibit at the 1904 World's Fair in St. Louis, Missouri. After the fair, still under armed guard, he joined a Wild West show.

Geronimo in 1903

In 1905 he rode a horse in President Theodore Roosevelt's **inaugural** parade. The old leader appeared not to mind the attention. He was admired by many now—and his fame was giving him much-needed income.

Now that Geronimo and other Indians were no longer a threat, Americans began to **romanticize** them. A belief in the "vanishing Indian" was common. Instead of treating Indians fairly, many people found it easier to think of them as being part of the past. They saw them as part of an era that was fading away.

inaugural—swearing in
romanticize—treat as idealized

Geronimo (second from right) rode in President Theodore Roosevelt's inaugural parade.

Geronimo (center) with his fighters

Effect #4: Geronimo as Legend

Today Geronimo has long been known to pop culture, appearing in movies, books, and comics. Some have painted him as a ruthless killer. Others have shown him in a kinder light.

"People tend to deal with Geronimo not as an actual person, but as an ideal," said Michael Darrow, the Fort Sill Apache tribal historian. "There was an **iconic** Geronimo. That's why when people ask me about Geronimo, I ask them if they are talking about Geronimo the person or Geronimo the myth."

iconic —widely viewed as perfectly capturing the meaning or spirit of something or someone

Code Name Geronimo

Geronimo's legendary name has also found an outlet in war. When plunging into battle during World War II, paratroopers traditionally cried "Geronimo!" to get their courage up.

More recently Geronimo was used as the code name for the capture of the al-Qaeda leader Osama bin Laden. In the early morning hours of May 2, 2011, U.S. Navy SEALS broke into a Pakistani compound and killed Osama bin Laden. The world's most wanted terrorist was behind the September 11, 2001, attacks on the twin towers of New York City's World Trade Center. U.S. Special Forces had been hunting him ever since. Now a sigh of relief sounded around the globe.

But along with relief came sadness and outrage from American Indians. The military had given the raid, and possibly bin Laden himself, the code name "Geronimo." American Indians called the use of Geronimo's name disrespectful. Many Indian leaders issued statements of disappointment and disapproval. They asked that the code name be changed.

Jeff Houser, tribal chairman of the Fort Sill Apache, asked for an apology in a letter to President Barack Obama. "Unlike the coward Osama bin Laden, Geronimo faced his enemy in numerous battles and engagements," Houser wrote. "He is perhaps one of the greatest symbols of Native American resistance in the history of the United States."

Congress Honors Geronimo

The Fort Sill Apache have their headquarters in the Oklahoma town of Apache. They maintain close ties to the Mescalero Apache in New Mexico.

As for Geronimo, February 17, 2009, was the 100th anniversary of his death. Later that month the U.S. House of Representatives passed a resolution that "honors the life of Goyathlay, his extraordinary bravery, and his commitment to the defense of his homeland, his people, and Apache ways of life." House Resolution 132 also acknowledged the many wrongdoings of the United States against Geronimo and the Apache people. Geronimo's life ensured that the struggles of the Apache will never be forgotten.

Geronimo posed for famed photographer Edward S. Curtis in 1905.

TIMELINE

Early 1820s:
Geronimo is born at the headwaters of the Gila River, near the border of Arizona and New Mexico.

March 4, 1851:
Geronimo loses his wife, children, and his mother in a massacre by Mexican forces.

1850s-1870s:
Geronimo leads a relentless campaign against Mexicans and American settlers trying to protect his people and their Apache homelands.

1872:
The U.S. government establishes the Chiricahua Reservation in southern Arizona and forces Geronimo and other Apache to live there.

1876:
The U.S. Army relocates Geronimo and his followers to the San Carlos Reservation in Arizona; a defiant Geronimo escapes and begins raiding from the Sierra Madre Mountains in Mexico.

April 21, 1877:
Geronimo is captured in Ojo Caliente and taken to live on the San Carlos Reservation.

1878:
Geronimo and his followers flee the reservation, returning in 1880. They leave again in 1881.

1882:
Geronimo and his followers attack the reservation and take hundreds of Apache with them.

September 3, 1886:
After a massive military hunt for the fugitive, Geronimo surrenders for the final time, to General Nelson A. Miles.

October 25, 1886:
After several weeks imprisoned in Texas, Geronimo and several other Apache prisoners of war are sent to Fort Pickens, Florida. Their families are sent to Fort Marion in Florida.

May 13, 1888:
Geronimo and other Apache prisoners are relocated to Mount Vernon Barracks in Alabama, where they are reunited with their families.

October 4, 1894:
Geronimo and 258 other prisoners of war are taken to Fort Sill in Oklahoma Territory.

1904:
Geronimo appears as a celebrity at the St. Louis World's Fair.

March 9, 1905:
A few days after appearing in President Theodore Roosevelt's inaugural parade, Geronimo pleads the case for his people to return to their Arizona homelands, but the president denies his request.

February 17, 1909:
Geronimo dies at Fort Sill, Oklahoma, and is buried in the Apache cemetery there.

February 23, 2009:
The U.S. House of Representatives passes Resolution 132 honoring Geronimo's life and acknowledging the wrongs done to him and his people.

GLOSSARY

band (BAND)—group of related people who live and hunt together

bounty (BAUN-tee)—money offered for killing or capturing someone

campaign (kam-PAYN)—series of battles fought in one region

custody (KUHS-tuh-dee)—imprisonment

frontier (fruhn-TIHR)—the far edge of a settled area, where few people live

hostage (HOSS-tij)—person taken by force and held, often as a way to obtain something

iconic (EYE-kon-ik)—widely viewed as perfectly capturing the meaning or spirit of something or someone

inaugural (in-AW-ger-ul)—swearing in

massacre (MASS-uh-kuhr)—the deliberate killing of a group of unarmed people

prophecy (PROF-eh-see)—something that a person says will happen in the future

prospector (PROSS-pekt-or)—person who looks for valuable minerals, especially silver and gold

ration (RASH-uhn)—a person's daily share of food

renegade (REN-uh-gade)—someone who rejects lawful behavior

reservation (rez-er-VAY-shuhn)—area of land set aside by the U.S. government for American Indians; in Canada reservations are called reserves

romanticize (ro-MAN-ta-size)—treat as idealized

scout (SKOWT)—someone who travels ahead of a military group to gather information about the enemy

READ MORE

Birchfield, D.L., and Helen Dwyer. *Apache History and Culture.* Native American Library. New York: Gareth Stevens Pub., 2012.

Collins, Terry. *Into the West: Causes and Effects of U.S. Westward Expansion.* North Mankato, Minn.: Capstone Press, 2014.

Spilsbury, Richard. *Geronimo.* Hero Journals. Chicago: Raintree, 2014.

INTERNET SITES

FactHound offers a safe, fun way to find Internet sites related to this book. All of the sites on FactHound have been researched by our staff.

Here's all you do:

Visit *www.facthound.com*

Type in this code: 9781491448366

Check out projects, games and lots more at
www.capstonekids.com

CRITICAL THINKING USING THE COMMON CORE

1. What reasons did the Apache have for continually raiding in the Southwest? Do you think their raids were justified? Why or why not? (Integration of Knowledge and Ideas)

2. Once Geronimo surrendered for the last time, why did the government keep him prisoner for the rest of his life? Do you think Geronimo would have lived peacefully if he had been allowed to return to his Arizona homelands? (Key Ideas and Details)

3. Examine the map on page 23. Which locations were the last three places Geronimo lived? What were conditions like for him? (Craft and Structure)

INDEX